So You Want To Work With

Computers?

Margaret McAlpine

HODDER
Wayland

an imprint of Hodder Children's Books

First published in 2004 by Hodder Wayland,
an imprint of Hodder Children's Books

© Hodder Wayland 2004

Editor: Laura Milne
Inside design: Peta Morey
Cover design: Hodder Wayland

British Library Cataloguing Publication Data

McAlpine, Margaret
So you want to work with computers?
1.Computer industry – Vocational guidance – Juvenile literature
2.Information technology – Vocational guidance – Juvenile literature
I.Title

ISBN 0 7502 4533 6

Printed in China by WKT Company Ltd.

Hodder Children's Books
A division of Hodder Headline Limited
338 Euston Road, London NW1 3BH

Picture Acknowledgements. The publishers would like to thank the following
for allowing their pictures to be reproduced in this publication:
Phil Banko/Corbis 19r; Brooklyn Productions/Corbis 29; Corbis: 9, 10, 13, 15,
16, 21, 24, 37, 39, 51, 56; Jim Craigmyle/Corbis 40; Darama/Corbis 44;
DiMaggio/Kalish/Corbis 43t; Paul Edmondson/Corbis 17; ER Productions/
Corbis 30; Randy Faris/Corbis 19l, 48; John Feingersh/Corbis 22, 49; Patrik
Giardino/Corbis 59r; Tom Grill/Corbis 35t; Walter Hodges/Corbis 23, 47; Ted
Horowitz/Corbis 55; JFPI Studios, Inc/Corbis 35b; Jose Luis Pelaez, Inc/Corbis
5, 6, 27t, 28, 32, 53; Catherine Karnow/Corbis 59l; Helen King/Corbis 33;
Andrew Kolesnikow, Elizabeth Whiting & Associates/Corbis 43b; Larry Williams
and Associates/Corbis 57; Lester Lefkowitz/Corbis 38; Left Lane Productions/
Corbis 31; Rob Lewine/Corbis 27b; Robert Maass/Corbis 45; Michael A Keller
Studios, Ltd/Corbis 52; Darren Modricker/Corbis 25; Paul Morris/Corbis 50;
Joaquin Palting/Corbis 7, 41; Picture Arts/Corbis 11, 20; Michael Pole/Corbis
54; Michael Prince/Corbis 46; Anthony Redpath/Corbis 12; Gerhard
Steiner/Corbis 4, 36; Bill Varie/Corbis 14; Tom Wagner/Corbis Saba 8.

Note: Photographs illustrating the 'day in the life of' pages are posed
by models.

weblinks

You don't need a computer to use this book. But, for readers who do have access to the Internet, the book provides links to recommended websites which offer additional information and resources on the subject.

You will find weblinks boxes like this on some pages of the book.

weblinks

For more IT careers advice, go to
www.waylinks.co.uk/
series/soyouwant/computers

waylinks.co.uk

To help you find the recommended websites easily and quickly, weblinks are provided on our own website, **waylinks.co.uk**. These take you straight to the relevant websites and save you typing in the Internet address yourself.

Internet safety

↗ Never give out personal details, which include: your name, address, school, telephone number, email address, password and mobile number.

↗ Do not respond to messages which make you feel uncomfortable – tell an adult.

↗ Do not arrange to meet in person someone you have met on the Internet.

↗ Never send your picture or anything else to an online friend without a parent's or teacher's permission.

↗ If you see anything that worries you, tell an adult.

A note to adults
Internet use by children should be supervised. We recommend that you install filtering software which blocks unsuitable material.

Website content

The weblinks for this book are checked and updated regularly. However, because of the nature of the Internet, the content of a website may change at any time, or a website may close down without notice. While the Publishers regret any inconvenience this may cause readers, they cannot be responsible for the content of any website other than their own.

HODDER
Wayland

Contents

Words in **bold** can be found in the glossary.

Games Designer

What is a games designer?

A games **designer** is a person who writes or creates the **software** used to play games on **personal computers** or popular games machines such as the Xbox.

Modern computer games are so advanced that games designers almost never work on their own. Instead they work as part of a games design team.

A huge variety of computer games are played regularly by a large number of people. So many different types of games are produced, there really is something for everybody.

There are several different **platforms** or game playing systems on the market, for which games are available, including:

- Home computer
- GameCube
- PlayStation
- Xbox.

Brainstorming sessions are often the first step in the games development process.

Gaming success

The video game industry is extremely profitable. At present, more money is being made from the sales of video games than is made from cinema box office sales. This means many people prefer to stay at home and play games than go out to see a film.

Artists' impressions of characters are made before the prototype (rough example) is written.

Even if the game is an exact copy of a game already available for use on a different platform it has to be rewritten in a new version for the new platform. Sometimes this rewrite involves a completely different **programming language**.

When a game sells well it is not unusual for designers to return to the program and make an 'extension pack'. These contain extra levels to the game and often introduce new characters.

weblinks

For more information on the history of computer games, go to www.waylinks.co.uk/series/soyouwant/computers

Main tasks of a games designer

A team of games designers discuss ideas for new games. They hold 'brainstorming' sessions where everyone suggests new ideas and concepts for new games.

Concepts for games are shown to a panel of experienced staff. If they like the idea, it is passed for further development.

An early stage of the project is making a prototype (rough example), to show the features of the game including:

● look or appearance of the game;
● main characters;
● movement of the characters;
● way in which the game is played.

The development process is always subject to change.

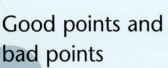

Good points and bad points

'Being a games designer means working with an imaginative group of people, who take ideas for new games and turn them into reality. It's also good to read a positive review of a game that I have worked on. Of course it's not so good if the review isn't a good one.'

Games developers create all the detailed stages of the game. This includes features such as:

- game environment or settings;
- speech used by characters;
- **user interface** or information as it appears on the screen;
- controls.

Writing the **code** enables the designer's ideas to become reality.

They break down the game storyline into stages before they begin to write the program with each stage becoming a game level.

Once the original copy is written, games designers oversee the testing of the game. This is done to make sure the game runs well on the platform for which it is written. Games designers must keep up to date with new **hardware** in order to write the best games.

A great number of changes or additions to the software are often needed as a result of the testing. This can make the design of a game very lengthy. It is possible for a game to spend many months in the design phase, with big games taking over a year to complete.

Once the game has been completed, designers have to write instruction manuals for the players to use.

Skills needed to be a games designer

Imagination
Games designers need to be creative and have a vivid imagination in order to think of new game concepts.

Flexibility
They must be flexible as the design process is always changing and the final version of the game can be quite different from the original idea.

Knowledge
In order to know what makes a successful game, designers must know all about the history of games and their development. A good knowledge of computers and their programming languages is also vital for games designers. This knowledge must be kept up to date all the time, so the games they produce are at the forefront of technology.

Analytical
Designers need well-developed analytical skills. There are often a lot of small problems that arise and have to be located and put right.

Play testing is a lengthy but necessary process.

Communication
Good communication within the design team is very important. Different members of the team are responsible for different aspects of the game such as character appearance, game controls or sound.

The final result is hours of fun.

All these different parts must fit together perfectly for the game to be a success, which means designers explaining to the rest of the team exactly what they are doing. There is no place for anyone who wants to work alone because the design process is too lengthy and complicated to be done by one person.

fact file

Games designers usually have a degree in a computer related subject. But what is more important is that they have the type of creative mind that can invent new games. The way in is often to find a job with a games company and work up to becoming a designer.

A day in the life of a games designer

Dave Alvarez

Dave is 29 years old and works for a games development company. He has been a games enthusiast for many years.

7.30 am   I'm on my way to work and I'm already thinking over some new ideas I have for a game.

8.30 am   I get into the office and read through my **emails**. If possible I reply to them right away. Otherwise I mark them for action later in the day.

9.00 am   At the moment we have just finished testing a PC-based game we are developing, for possible issues with **compatibility**. These happen when a piece of software doesn't work with certain pieces of hardware.

The testing has been going on for some time and I enter the results into a **database** ready for a development team meeting.

11.00 am   Having entered as many results as possible into the database, I now need to create presentation aids for the development meeting this afternoon. Fortunately for me, the database automatically produces figures from my **data** and then turns them into lots of attractive charts and graphs.

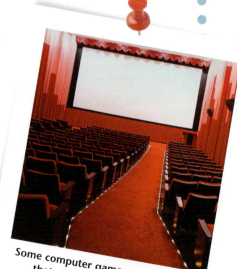

Some computer games are so popular that they are made into films.

A busy day can often mean working through lunch.

12.00 pm In theory this is my lunch break but I spend it working on my figures and responding to any outstanding emails.

1.00 pm Time for the development team meeting. I show other members of the team the results of the compatibility tests and we discuss which problems are the most urgent.

We consider what we can do to solve them and whether this could have any knock-on effect on the game. We also decide exactly who is responsible for making any changes to the game.

5.00 pm I switch off my desktop computer. Then I find myself sketching out some of those ideas I had this morning on the way to work.

Hardware Engineer

What is a hardware engineer?

Hardware engineers are responsible for the updating, **maintenance** and repair of computer systems. The hardware is the computing system itself and all the different parts that make it up such as the **network server**, work stations and **Internet** connection equipment (modems).

Large companies that have their own IT (information technology) department and large computer systems may have their own 'in house' team of hardware engineers. Having their own engineers means that any problems that arise can be dealt with as soon as possible.

Freelance engineers travel to the sites of individual clients who require their skills. Some hardware engineers travel to locations all around the country and abroad. Work on a site may last from one or two days to a month or more.

The development of bigger and better software applications means they cannot be run on older and slower computer systems. These systems need to be updated perhaps by increasing storage capacity or adding peripheral (external) hardware such as **scanners** to the system.

A high level of technical knowledge is needed to work as a hardware engineer.

Computers through the ages

In 1943 the chairman of IBM, now one of the world's leading computer manufacturers, believed there was a world market potential for 'maybe five computers'. By the 1960s leading engineers were quoted as saying in the future it might be possible to produce computers weighing no more than 1.5 tons.

Today computer systems are small and light enough to fit inside wrist watches and mobile phones.

In some cases old systems need to be replaced completely. As hardware grows older it becomes more likely to break down. When a system needs to be replaced altogether, the hardware engineer will write a report and present it to the management and financial departments, and together they will make the decision.

No job is too big or too small.

Hardware engineers working within an organisation work shifts and spend some time on call, ready to answer out-of-hours emergencies.

Main tasks of a hardware engineer

Hardware engineers calculate the cost of **upgrades** to computer systems. This involves:

- Examining the hardware already used by the company at the site.
- Checking to see if an upgrade or the addition of new equipment is required.
- Trying to find the most effective way of updating the system.
- Deciding whether the entire system needs to be replaced.

Should a piece of equipment be broken, hardware engineers must locate the problem with the hardware as quickly as possible because broken computer systems cost companies a great deal of money in lost work time.

Being on call means the day can be a long one.

Good points and bad points

'The best part of my job is knowing exactly how the different parts of a computer work together. As a hardware engineer I make sure that systems are working properly. Often I am faced with problems that are not easy to solve. However, in these cases it's very rewarding when I do find the answer.'

Hardware engineers are constantly having to keep up with new technology.

Hardware engineers often work with financial **analysts**. The equipment they are repairing is often very expensive so they must prove that the benefits of the work they are doing will be worth the cost. Analysts help in these calculations.

Once they have been given the go-ahead for the work they have suggested, the engineer is responsible for the **installation** of the new hardware. This stage of the project may take some time, especially if a large network is being replaced.

The project doesn't necessarily finish with the installation of a new piece of hardware. Hardware engineers may have to return to the site in order to deal with compatibility issues, which can occur when certain pieces of hardware do not work well together. These stop the system working properly but may only be noticed after the company has been using the new system for some time.

Skills needed to be a hardware engineer

Knowledge

Hardware engineers need very good technical knowledge in order to be able to work with complicated computer systems. They also have to spend time keeping up with developments because the world of **information technology** is always changing.

Analytical

They need very good analytical skills in order to work out what is wrong on very advanced systems. In the case of upgrades to clients' systems, they have to examine the requirements of the software that the clients wish to use and choose just the right upgrades to do this.

Hardware engineers often work as part of a small team on projects.

Time management

Hardware engineers often work to deadlines set by the clients. These can be very tight which means that engineers have to be committed to their work and be prepared to work long hours to get a job finished on time.

Flexibility

Work on computer systems often changes a great deal between the planning and the final stages. For this reason flexibility is an important quality for hardware engineers who have to adapt to changes.

Communication

Hardware engineers have to discuss their plans in detail with several groups such as business analysts and technical salespeople. This means they need to have good communication skills.

Organisation

Self-employed hardware engineers need to build up their own network of clients in order to stay in business. They have to be well organised, contact clients swiftly and make sure the standard of their work is so high that clients return to them with more business.

Investigation is the first step. Then the action follows.

fact file

Most hardware engineers have qualifications such as National Vocational Qualifications (NVQs), General National Vocational Qualifications (GNVQs), City & Guilds or BTECs. Some take a degree in computer science or engineering. An important entry route is with an employer through a Foundation or Advanced Modern Apprenticeship.

weblinks

For more information on working as a hardware engineer, go to www.waylinks.co.uk/series/soyouwant/computers

A day in the life of a hardware engineer

Dennis Chung

Dennis is a hardware engineer, working for a company that provides support to organisations experiencing problems with their computer systems.

8.30 am   I spend my spare time before being called out checking messages and keeping up to date with new hardware and software developments.

9.00 am   A customer phones, telling me that all is well with some repair work I carried out yesterday. He seems to be happy, which is a relief. I respond to some emailed requests and make a couple of phone calls.

10.00 am   A call from a customer who runs the computer department of an engineering factory. He has a problem with his **floppy disc drive**. I come up with some ideas and suggest a solution. Some queries we can deal with over the phone, but I spend a lot of time working on customers' premises.

10.30 am   This could be a big one. A major customer has reported a problem with their £2 million hardware system.

            We have different agreements with customers, regarding our response levels. These vary from a 24 hour response time, which means we have to be dealing with the problem in that time, to an agreement to have a problem fixed in a few hours.

11.00 am I'm in my car and on my way, armed with my toolbox, which I take on every job. I open up computers and approach the repair in the same way as an electrician would repair a fridge or a washing machine. I also have with me a set of CDs which I put in to the computer to help me **diagnose** what is wrong.

2.00 pm I'm getting there, but it's a long job. I also have to spend time reassuring the staff that I know what I'm doing.

4.15 pm Back to my office to write a report on the problem I've just solved and to check if my customer has sorted out his difficulties with his floppy disc.

6.00 pm I close my office, taking the pager with me as tonight I'm on call for emergencies.

Hardware engineers must know a great deal about all sorts of computer components.

Server rooms like this are a common sight today.

Helpdesk Professional

What is a helpdesk professional?

A helpdesk professional's job is to answer questions from people who ask for help with either their computer hardware or with the software they are using. Usually the helpdesk professional listens to the description of the problem and then suggests a method of solving it. Most often this is done by giving step-by-step instructions over the phone.

There are different types of helpdesk professional:

- Companies that produce software applications need helpdesk professionals to support first time users who are having difficulty installing the software or are unsure how to operate it.
- In companies that produce computer hardware, problems may arise when customers try to install the hardware into their computer system. They need a helpdesk professional to solve them.
- An in-house helpdesk professional supports large **networks** of computers such as those found in companies, universities or government departments. In this situation the helpdesk professional responds mainly to telephone enquiries from staff in the same company experiencing all kinds of problems, from computers that keep **crashing**, to a broken mouse.

Helpdesk professionals deal with many calls in a day.

Sometimes a visit is needed to solve a problem.

The computer boom

40 years ago there were only six computers in the world. Today there is scarcely an organisation anywhere that does not rely on **information technology** in some form or other.

Most of the enquiries a helpdesk professional receives are answered over the phone. Some enquiries may be too complicated to deal with by phone, particularly if the caller is not confident with computers. In cases such as these the helpdesk professional may go to the caller's desk and help them face-to-face.

weblinks

For the British Computer Society's website, go to www.waylinks.co.uk/series/soyouwant/computers

Main tasks of a helpdesk professional

Clients contact the helpdesk professional in a number of ways, for example by phone, **email**, fax or sometimes in person, to discuss the problems that they are experiencing. It is important that the helpdesk professionals are easy to contact so they can deal with the problems quickly and efficiently.

Helpdesk professionals must record all their calls.

An important part of the helpdesk professional's role is to investigate the problem that their clients are experiencing. Helpdesk professionals must ask the caller a series of direct questions in order to find out the nature of the problems. In most cases they do not actually see the caller's computer system.

Good points and bad points

'I like the level of contact I have with people and enjoy being able to help them with their problems. The only drawback I find about my job is some people are angry even before they call. Usually this is caused by their confusion and frustration, and by the time the call has finished they are happy again.'

When the nature of the problem has been investigated, the helpdesk professionals can begin to suggest solutions to the problem. Usually they give their callers step-by-step instructions to help clients to solve their problem. Instructions are given over the phone. If they are complicated they will also be sent by fax or email to make sure the details are given to the client correctly.

Helpdesk professionals provide a great deal of after-sales information for the companies they work for. They record the problems clients have encountered from all of the calls that they receive.

When helpdesk professionals record the subject of each call, a body of **data** accumulates about what problems are occurring. This data is then used by others to upgrade and redesign products to eliminate common problems.

Helpdesk professionals are happy to give general advice to staff about using their computers.

Skills needed to be a helpdesk professional

Quick thinking
Helpdesk professionals often have to speak to people who are unhappy or angry. In these cases the operator must be able to think swiftly to make sure that the client's problems are solved as quickly as possible.

Knowledge
It is very important that helpdesk professionals know a great deal about the software or the hardware with which they are dealing.

Communication
They have to speak clearly and simply and know the right questions to ask of people in order to find out the problem and solve it. Sometimes a caller will say they have done something when they haven't, so helpdesk professionals have to come up with new ways of asking the same question.

Helpdesk areas in some companies are very big and employ a lot of people.

Good listeners
Helpdesk professionals must be good listeners as they are often dealing with non-technical people who do not fully understand what they are doing. It is important that they are able to interpret exactly what the caller is saying.

Friendly
A friendly manner is important, as helpdesk professionals must remain calm and tactful when

Helpdesk professionals are responsible for helping all members of staff who use a computer.

dealing with all their callers, even those who are upset and not explaining very clearly what is wrong.

Professional
Customer care is an important part of the helpdesk professional's job. They are often a caller's first point of contact with a company. It is important that callers feel they are being given a high level of service so they remain confident in the company and its products.

fact file

Most helpdesk professionals go into the work after they have gained experience of their employer's computer system and the way in which the business is run, through doing a different job in the computer department.

Some employers ask for a degree or a BTEC qualification while others are less concerned about qualifications and offer their own training.

A day in the life of a helpdesk professional

Kathryn Dean

Kathryn is a helpdesk professional in a large government office.

8.00 am	I arrive in the office bright and early. This way I am in before the other members of staff and I can be set up and ready before anyone starts to have problems.
8.30 am	I put on my headset and start to answer incoming calls from members of staff. Some of their calls are really quite short, while others take longer to deal with than they should.
	While I'm listening to the call I record everything on the system so that we can keep records of what seems to be going wrong.
11.00 am	In between telephone calls I check my **email** for requests for help. Email requests tend to be either a little less urgent than phone requests or a lot more complicated. From my point of view this makes answering email requests more interesting.
	Unfortunately while doing this I still have to answer the phone so I have to be able to keep lots of different things in my mind at the same time.
12.30 pm	Lunch.
1.30 pm	Having written rough answers to the more detailed problems that I have received in my email inbox this morning, I now check them and send them off to the people who sent the enquiries. While I'm doing this I have to answer any incoming phone queries.

2.30 pm   I go to see the people who have problems and need me to visit their desks, to offer a solution. This may be because the answer to the problem is complicated, or it may be because I need to mend some part of the computer itself. Afterwards it's back to my desk to deal with more calls.

5.30 pm   People are leaving the building and I can think about going home.

Sometimes a problem can have a simple solution.

It can be difficult remembering everything.

Software Developer

What is a software developer?

Software is the name given to programs that run on a computer system. Software developers (sometimes called computer programmers) design and create the programs.

Some software developers work in **corporate**/business software development, which means they create software that is used by companies in the daily running of their business. Software can include billing systems for banks and research projects for universities.

There are two different types of developer:

- In-house developers are employed by a company and may be involved with many different departments within that company.
- **Independent** developers work from their own offices and may have several different companies as clients.

Software developers create software solutions for people in many different industries.

Software developers meet and talk to their clients to find out exactly what they need the new program to do before they create the software.

Today nearly all companies rely on different software programs to help them to conduct business which means software developers are found in all areas of work.

Software problems

Japanese researchers have shown that nearly 37% of the faults that are recorded in new software releases could be avoided if the developers had been given more time in which to finish the product.

Many people have computers at home and every program that runs on those systems will have been designed by a software development team. These types of programs are known as **end-user** programs because they are used by individuals, not companies.

Software developers also work for huge multinational companies employing thousands of staff. At one time so many of these computer companies were based in an area of California that it became known as Silicon Valley.

Freelance developers may need to work away from home.

Network software developers create software that helps computers communicate with each other as part of a network, more quickly and effectively.

Research and development software is often developed especially for different university research projects to carry out advanced research work.

Main tasks of a software developer

Most software developers, whether working in-house or independently, work as part of a team including other software developers and software analysts. Software developers work alongside analysts to look at the problems the new software is intended to solve so they can come up with a **cost-effective** solution for the client.

They often need to get to know their clients' business in detail. This means that developers spend a lot of time with their clients. Independent software developers often travel to clients and work away from home for short periods of time.

Developers present their ideas to **management** teams. They may be asked to explain in great detail why they have chosen certain solutions over others.

Clients need to be kept up to date with new developments.

Good points and bad points

'Working as part of a small team is great and the feeling you get at the end of a project when your program is up and running is amazing. The only drawback I can think of is the long hours we often put in as a team as we approach the deadline.'

After deciding upon the exact requirements of the software, the program code is written. Writing program codes used to take a long time, but now CASE (Computer Assisted Software Engineering) programs assist in the process and it is often **automated**. This means the program translates the programmer's instructions into code.

Testing is an important part of the development process. Detailed testing of the program is necessary to make sure that it works as it should on all the computer systems.

The final stage of the development process is the writing of technical manuals and instruction books. It is very important that these are written in a way that is easy to understand as future users of the software may not be familiar with computers.

Developers help to train clients in the use of new software.

weblinks

For general information on working in IT, go to www.waylinks.co.uk/series/ soyouwant/computers

Skills needed to be a software developer

Knowledge

Software developers need to have a high level of knowledge and be experts in the latest software and hardware solutions. Programming or the actual writing of program code may form an important part of the software developer's job – in this case it is important that they have an excellent knowledge of the computer language they intend to use.

There's always something new to learn.

Good presentation

They need to have good presentation skills so that they can put over ideas to customers and create detailed instructions for new users.

Numerate

Software developers need to be good with numbers, especially those involved in research software development. They may have to write programs to carry out complicated mathematical operations.

Analytical

Good analytical skills are needed to enable software developers to examine the nature of the problems they are trying to solve and to work out exactly what is required of the software they are developing.

Writing programming codes can be a lengthy business.

Communication

Getting on with people is important because developers have to talk to clients about what exactly they want and how best this can be done.

Teamwork

Teamwork skills are necessary as developers usually work as part of a small group of people from different job areas. It is important that they are all able to work together.

fact file

A growing number of people take the graduate entry into **information technology** with a degree in a computer related subject.

Once in a job, short training courses are usually offered to software developers to make sure they keep up with new developments in information technology.

A day in the life of a software developer

David Nugent

David is a senior software developer with a company designing and developing new software.

9.00 am   I get into work and set up my **workstation**. I usually have half an hour to check my **emails** and get ready for my first appointment.

9.30 am   Team meeting to discuss developments within one of our projects. These meetings often involve looking at possible new answers to problems that have come up.

11.00 am   Meeting with analysts and possible new clients to discuss what they are looking for. This went on for longer than intended as the clients didn't realise the difficulties involved in what they wanted.

1.00 pm   I usually allow myself half an hour for lunch, which I often have to eat on the run.

1.30 pm   My next job is overseeing **construction**. We have a team of programmers who work on the program code for us. It is my job to review the program code that has been written, to make sure things are going well. In addition to that I may spend some of the afternoon going over testing results with the programmers to check that things are working well during the testing process.

3.30 pm   I review the progress of the day and check on emails received since the morning. Then I answer the rest of my mail and update my diary for future appointments.

5.00 pm   Time to pack up.

(The day I have described is a fairly relaxed one. As we approach a deadline I may well remain in the office until 7.30 or 9.00 pm.)

Client meetings are important, to find out exactly what is required of the new software.

Software developers need to be in touch with many different people.

Systems Analyst

What is a systems analyst?

Systems analysts look into a business problem from both a technical and **commercial** point of view. They then look at computer systems and the ways in which these could be used and developed in order to solve the problem.

Any organisations including banks, supermarkets or government departments that have a large computer network, need a systems analyst. Usually systems analysts work in an office. If they are self-employed they may work in their client's offices for a length of time.

Systems analysts work alongside staff from many different departments.

The importance of computers

Companies are investing heavily in computers. In 1990 worldwide company investment in computer systems stood for 20% of their total investment programme. By the year 2000 this figure had doubled to 40% of all new investment.

There are many different areas in which analysts work. One of the growing areas is **e-commerce**. This is the name given to business carried on over the Internet.

One of the most important parts of an e-commerce systems analyst's job is to make sure that clients are linked correctly to a company's **internal network** to enable them to do business with each other.

Analysts meet and work alongside many different people in their job. They work with:

- Management teams to discuss the aims of the project.
- Information security teams to make sure a new system is secure.
- Network operations to check that the new system will work properly with the existing one.
- Software developers who are responsible for creating changes in the present software or writing new software.

Preparation before a meeting is vital.

weblinks

For more information on working as a systems analyst, go to www.waylinks.co.uk/series/soyouwant/computers

Main tasks of a systems analyst

Systems analysts create solutions to what may be complicated business or technical problems.

They draw up detailed plans for an **upgraded** or new computer system. They work out the cost of a project and compare it to the benefits the project will bring, to see if it is worth making the changes to the system.

They work together with **programmers**, designers and other skilled staff, to make sure that the planned changes work well and that clients get what they want.

Analysts help to train staff in the use of their new system.

They draw up a work plan that has to include time for the development process, design and application to make sure projects are completed by the deadline date.

Good points and bad points

'The part I like most about my job is working with the internet security team. It gives me great satisfaction to know that once I have created a new computer system it is safe from attack by anyone outside the company. One drawback of the job can be the time some problems take to solve.'

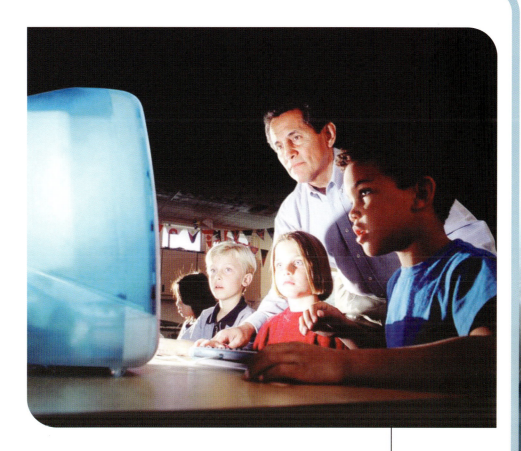

Security has become an important part of IT work and it often falls to the analysts working with security experts to make sure that the information held on a system is safe from **hackers** who may want to break into the system.

Systems analysts draw up a **test plan** for each system (to ensure that there are no problems in its operation that have not been considered). They also manage the **installation** of a new system to make sure that it is installed or put in correctly.

Their final task is to make sure that training and instruction manuals are correctly written and printed so staff are able to use the system properly.

Installation projects may be big or small.

Skills needed to be a systems analyst

Knowledge
Analysts need a high level of technical knowledge in both software and hardware so that they can work out what areas are in need of change.

Logic
Analysts have to be able to investigate problems in a logical step-by-step manner, to find out where possible problems in the planned system may lie.

The project goes through several changes before its completion.

Business sense
It is very important for analysts to have a strong understanding of the business they are working in, in order to judge the needs of their client. Often self-employed analysts specialise in particular fields such as banking or **manufacturing**.

Analysts often work to strict deadlines.

Communication

Strong communication skills are very important for analysts as they must be able to give information in a clear, simple way to people who have no technical knowledge of computers.

Patience

Analysts may experience some difficulties from company staff about the changes they plan to make to a computer system. In cases like this they need tact and patience to explain the advantages of their ideas and persuade people to accept the new system.

fact file

The most usual way to become a systems analyst is with a degree or Higher National Diploma (HND) or Higher National Certificate (HNC). Companies do take people with a degree in a non-computer related subject and offer them training.

The computer industry tends to be quite flexible about qualifications and employers often prefer experience in the job rather than a particular qualification.

A day in the life of a systems analyst

Jasmeena Mistri

Jasmeena is 27 years old and works as a systems analyst.

9.00 am   I arrive at work and go to my desk, usually by way of the coffee machine. I **boot up** my machine, check my **emails** and then go to my diary software in order to check my appointments for the day.

9.30 am   My first appointment is a team meeting to review the plans for a new sales network we are designing for a financial institution. At this meeting we try to work out the possible cost of developing two designs we have created.

11.30 am   I have a meeting with business analysts to discuss the possible costs of the project. We look at the cost of making one of the two designs and compare it to the **profits** the client will make. The business analysts have a clearer idea than I do of the cost benefit of the project.

1.00 pm   We carry on with the meeting and I have a **working lunch** with members of the business analysis team.

2.15 pm   I meet with members of the systems analysis team to discuss possible changes to the suggested designs. We have to think about putting in changes because the business analysis team feels that without them the project would be too expensive.

           The most common changes are made to save costs and keep the project within the client's **budget**.

4.45 pm   I compose and send emails containing all the suggested design changes to everyone concerned. The information will be with them first thing tomorrow morning and I have asked them to get back to me as soon as possible.

5.30 pm   I turn off my computer and head for home.

Analysts often work long hours to meet deadlines.

Analysts usually work in a modern office environment.

Technical Sales Specialist

What is a technical sales specialist?

Technical sales specialists work for companies that produce either hardware or software for computer systems. It is their job to sell their company's products to **information technology** companies, to computer departments in other companies and to any organisation that could be interested in their products.

The role of a technical sales specialist is in many ways similar to that of all sales people, whether the products they are selling are holidays, windows or cars.

Sales targets are an important part of any technical sales specialist's work.

Targeting the market

Individual users account for only about one third of computer sales. The majority of computers are bought by **commercial** organisations, government departments, universities and schools. Most businesses have reached the point where there is a workstation for every employee.

However, in such a technically advanced field it is very important that technical sales specialists fully understand the products they are selling, in order to explain their possible benefits to a client.

Clients need detailed **costings** before deciding whether to buy.

Technical sales specialists sell products worth millions of pounds, for example software to help a bank monitor **cash flow** and deliveries throughout its branches. It is the technical sales specialist's job to convince technical representatives at the bank that the new software is better than the system they have in place at the moment and that it would save them money in the long run.

In technical sales, the cost of the products and the complicated jobs they do mean that the sales specialists often put a great deal of work into getting the sale. Sometimes the sales process will happen over a period of weeks or months.

Main tasks of a technical sales specialist

Technical sales specialists are often given an area or region of the country for which they are responsible, and where they sell their company's products. They sell hardware which is the computing system itself, or software which is the systems run on the computer.

Technical sales specialists can spend a great deal of time travelling.

The products sold by technical sales specialists can offer very complicated solutions to meet a company's needs; for example, a computer system for a chain of international hotels, to enable staff to make bookings across the world. This makes it essential for sales specialists to know their clients' businesses really well.

Good points and bad points

'I am very much a people person which is why I work in sales. My job means I meet and talk to lots of different people. Working in technical sales is particularly good because it allows me to use my technical knowledge, in a sociable environment.'

'I like the satisfaction of meeting my sales target, although I often need to work long hours and don't have much free time.'

In order to be able to sell such sophisticated products,
technical sales specialists need a high level of
computer knowledge.

One of their first jobs is to maintain the **client base**
for the company within their area. To do this they
remain in regular contact with clients after a sale.
This contact:

- Helps to keep the customers loyal to the sales
  specialist's company.
- Offers an opportunity for the sales specialists to
  introduce new products to existing clients.

They are also responsible for expanding their client
base which means bringing in new business to the
company from within their area. This is done by
contacting potential clients by phone, **email** or in
person to arrange appointments when they can
explain or demonstrate new hardware or software.

Skills needed to be a technical sales specialist

Friendly

It is important for technical sales specialists to get on well with all types of people and to have a warm friendly approach to everyone.

Communication

Sales specialists need to give presentations to clients to show them the benefits of the product they are trying to sell. For this reason they need to be able to speak in a clear, interesting way and to explain complicated points as simply as possible.

A technical sales specialist meets a new client.

Business sense

Good business sense is important to technical sales specialists so they have a good idea how much a client will pay and can put together a sales deal that pleases the seller and the buyer.

Technical knowledge

Sales specialists have to talk to and deal with technical staff during the sale and so need to have a strong understanding of IT systems in general and of their particular products in order to get the sale they want.

The client's needs are discussed.

Confidence

Sales work requires sales specialists to 'close a deal'. This means convincing clients to buy their product. Good sales skills and confidence are vital if technical sales specialists are to be successful at work.

Optimism

Sales work will always involve contact with people who in the end decide not to buy the product. It is important for technical sales specialists not to let these occasions depress them and to have a positive and cheerful outlook on life.

fact file

Technical sales specialists usually have an HND or a degree in a computing subject.

Some move into sales from a technical job in design or production. Coming in to sales this way means they have very good knowledge of their company's products.

weblinks

For more IT career advice, go to www.waylinks.co.uk/series/soyouwant/computers

A day in the life of a technical sales specialist

Alison O'Rourke

Alison is a technical sales specialist for a **multinational** software company.

7.15 am My day starts early as I have to drive from my home to a sales appointment several miles away.

9.30 am I arrive at my appointment a quarter of an hour early. I do this on purpose as every salesman knows that there is no worse way to start a sales meeting than by being late. If you are late for an appointment it makes you look as if you're not particularly interested in the client.

9.45 am I give a half hour presentation to the client's management team to show what our software can do for their company. Once I have finished we spend time discussing the ways in which we can make our software meet their particular business needs. This may be done in a number of ways such as adapting the software to run on their computer systems or adding new **fields** to the software to adapt to their way of doing business.

Some meetings are held over lunch.

Technical sales specialists undergo a great deal of training.

12.00 pm   I have lunch with the clients and we continue to talk about the ways in which we can help them to conduct their business more quickly and profitably.

1.30 pm   I start the drive back to the office.

2.45 pm   I get back to the office, check my **emails** and catch up on my missed phone calls.

3.30 pm   I chat to the **software** development team and tell them about the changes that were suggested during my morning meeting with the client.

5.00 pm   I get in my car and drive back home, taking some paperwork with me. This evening I shall be preparing a report for my clients on the possible changes to their software.

Website Developer

What is a website developer?

Website developers design websites for people to visit through the Internet.

Through meeting with their clients they decide exactly what kind of information and features their client needs to display on their website. For example, a bank wants to show information such as interest rates, while a nightclub wants to show details of new events and guest performers.

Website developers not only need to decide on the wording of the site but also need to make it look attractive to the visitor. This means they have to know how to design an attractive layout. The appearance of the site is often decided by the type of business and the job it is needed to do. For example, government departments need a more formal site than a music store.

Websites have to be attractive to the people who visit them.

Who wants to be a millionaire?

The 40 richest millionaires and billionaires in the USA made their money through the Internet. In Australia nearly 200 new millionaires are created every week through association with the Internet.

Often website developers work in a design agency, as part of a small design team. These agencies work with a wide variety of clients, especially as a growing number of businesses discover the advantages of being on the web. Other website developers are self-employed and have any number of different clients.

Clients need to be kept up to date with progress.

Website developers also update sites. Customers return to website developers for additions and changes to their original site. This could be the addition of **e-commerce** facilities to sites, for instance, an online catalogue and the means for buying goods (maybe flights and holidays) through the website.

Main tasks of a website developer

The first stage of a website developer's work is to meet with clients to find out exactly what they expect from their website. Topics covered during this meeting are likely to include:

- Who is the site for?
- Why is it needed?
- What ideas does the client particularly want to see on the site?
- How much time does the design team have to create the site?
- How much money can the client spend?

Today you can book your holiday online.

Good points and bad points

'Recently, many different people have begun to see that a website can help them, making my job very interesting. Universities, travel companies, hotels and banks all have their own websites.

Sometimes it can be hard work persuading clients to make the best use of their website, because they don't understand what is possible and also have a limited amount of money to spend.'

The developers then create a draft or example site
for the clients to view. The developers write the code
for this and choose the programming languages they
will use:

- **HTML** or hyper text mark up language is the classic
  web design language and is well known and simple
  to use. However, web pages written only in this
  language often appear plain by today's standards.
- Modern programming languages such as Javascript
  allow for increasingly interesting web pages to be
  built with a more complicated site design that is
  attractive to people visiting the site.

Clients are given the opportunity to view the site
and to discuss it with the developer. This includes
talking about what they do not like and want to
have changed.

Once the final site has been completed and approved
by the client, the web development team **upload** the
site to a server. This is a computer that allows **web
browsers** to access the information it holds by way of
the Internet.

Skills needed to be a website developer

Creativity

Web design companies often prefer to employ someone with artistic skills as these people are able to create attractive sites. In the future this may become even more important, as programs are written that automate the writing of code for the website, leaving more time for the creative process. However at the moment web developers need to write the code for themselves.

Websites are designed for people in different kinds of industries.

Technical knowledge

More powerful programming languages are always being created, which makes the work more complicated. A high level of computer skills is essential for website developers.

Teamwork

Website developers need to work well with other people as they usually work in teams.

Most schools have their own website.

Presentation skills
Web developers need to be able to present draft ideas to their clients in meetings and to sell ideas to clients. They need to speak confidently and present information in a clear, interesting way.

Literate
Web developers contact clients in writing and write reports on the progress of the work, so they need to be able to write well.

fact file

This is a relatively new area and is developing very quickly. Employers are often flexible about qualifications. They may be looking for graduates, but most importantly they want creative employees who are capable of learning new skills and keeping up to date with new technology.

A day in the life of a website developer

Paula James

Paula is a website developer with a small web development company.

8.00 am   I like to be in early as my present role involves a lot of responsibility and design projects seem to be able to spring problems at me from many different directions. I reply to any **emails** that have been received and plan for the day.

9.00 am   I gather the design team for a meeting first thing in the morning. There are four of us and today we need to bring each other up to date on the progress we have each made on our part of a website development plan.

We also have our first coffee of the day. Coffee usually plays an essential part in the development process.

10.30 am   The next two hours are spent making the last-minute changes that have been agreed during the morning's meeting. Usually there are quite a lot of them.

12.30 pm   Lunch.

1.15 pm   I give a presentation. As the new team leader it usually falls to me to give presentations on draft sites to the customer.

Draft sites are simplified examples of the final sites. They allow the customer to get an idea of how the finished site will look. This is one of the most important parts of my job. I must make sure that the customer understands exactly what is happening on the site and ensure that we have done all that was needed of us.

3.00 pm The team meets up again to discuss the outcome of the meeting. These post-presentation meetings have been known to last for five hours if there is a great deal of change to be made to meet clients' wishes. Today it was quite a short meeting and only lasted two and a half hours.

5.30 pm After the last meeting I tidy up before leaving the office.

Clients need to understand how their website operates.

Getting together and sharing ideas is very helpful.

weblinks

For a case study of a website manager, go to www.waylinks.co.uk/series/soyouwant/computers

Glossary

analyst – a person who looks at a problem and breaks it down into logical steps.

automated – running a process on a computer, rather than using people.

boot up – when a computer is turned on and the operating applications automatically start to run. This process is called booting up.

budget – the amount of money that can be spent on a given project or program.

cash flow – the rate at which money enters or leaves a business.

client – a person or organisation for whom a piece of work is carried out.

client base – a list of the people or organisations which give work to a company.

code – term given to a computer programming language.

commerce/commercial – business/business surroundings.

compatibility – the ability of different pieces of equipment to work with each other.

construction – making or building something new.

corporate – large companies.

cost effective – saving or making money.

costing – working out the price of a job.

crashing – when a computer stops working in the middle of being used it is said to have crashed.

data – information held on computers.

database – computer system that contains information about a given subject. This could be a list of names and addresses or of company products.

designer – person who creates the plans for computer systems or programs.

diagnose – find the cause of a problem by looking at the symptoms.

e-commerce – business that is conducted over the Internet.

email – electronic contact between computers.

end-user – person or organisation that finally operates a product.

field – a space on a computer screen into which information is to be added.

floppy disk drive – the part of the computer into which disks are inserted to transfer information.

freelance – self employed people who work for themselves often carrying out work for more than one person or company.

hacker – a person who breaks into computer systems using the Internet.

hardware – physical parts of a computer system.

HTML – language used to create web pages.

independent – working or standing alone.

information technology – the name given to computing and computers.

installation – the setting up of either a program, network, or hardware into a system that already exists.

internal network – an organisation or department with its own linked system of computers.

Internet – an international network of computers linked up to exchange information.

maintenance – the upkeep and servicing of systems to make sure they operate well.

management – the organisation of workers and the overseeing of their work.

manufacturing – creating products from raw materials.

multinational – an activity involving more than just one country.

network – a group of computers joined or linked together so that they can share information.

network server – the main computer which organises contact between linked computers.

personal computer – machine used by one person.

platforms – computer operating systems.

profit – the money made by selling a product or service for more than the amount spent on producing it.

programmer – person who writes programs for computer systems.

programming language – a way of passing instructions into a machine.

scanner – hardware which can copy the image on any paper placed in it and turn the image into information that can be understood by a computer.

software – instructions to the computer which enable it to carry out a function for the operator.

teamwork – a group of people working together closely on a project.

test plan – a project designed to make sure that a program or system works properly without any problems.

upgrade – a new piece of hardware added to a computer system to improve it.

upload – installation of a piece of software to a system.

user interface – the way the person on the computer communicates with it, possibly by a keyboard or even a microphone.

web browser – a piece of software which interprets and reads website material.

website – space on the Internet owned by a person or an organisation.

working lunch – midday meal break spent working as well as eating.

workstation – a personal computer used in the workplace.

Further Information

So do you still want to work with computers?

Computers have changed the world in a very short space of time.

Today there are a growing number of jobs in the **information technology** or computer industry: either for specialist IT companies or in IT departments in hospitals, hotels, universities, and industrial and commercial organisations.

This book tries to show the wide range of different jobs that are available and to make it clear that girls enjoy working with computers just as much as boys.

There are far too many jobs working in computers to cover them all in this book. Just a few that have been left out are systems technician, call desk operator and operations manager.

The way to find out more about opportunities for working with computers is to read more books and to talk to people who are in that area of work.

If you are at secondary school and seriously interested in a career in computers, ask your careers teacher if he or she could arrange for some work experience. This means spending some time, usually a week or two in a computer environment.

Books

If you want to find out more about working with computers, you will find the following helpful:

Degree Course Guide: Computer Science and Computing, published by Hobsons, 1997.

Game Programming for Teens, by Maneesh Sethi, published by Course Technology Paperback, 2003.

Look Ahead: A Guide to Working in IT, by Deborah Fortune, published by Heinemann Library, 2001.

weblinks

For websites relevant to this book, go to
www.waylinks.co.uk/series/
soyouwant/computers

Useful addresses

Games Designer

Chartered Society of
Designers
32-38 Saffron Hill
London
EC1N 8FN
Tel: 0207 831 9777

Systems Analyst

Institution of Analysts &
Programmers
36 Culmington Road
London
W13 9NH
Tel: 0208 567 2118

Website Developer

British Interactive Media
Association (BIMA)
Briarlea House
Southend Road
South Green
Billericay
CM11 2PR
Tel: 01277 658107

*Contact the following
organisations for more
general information on
working with computers:*

British Computer Society
1 Sanford Street
Swindon
Wiltshire
SN1 1HJ
Tel: 01793 417417

E-skills UK
1 Castle Lane
London
SW1E 6DR
Tel: 0207 963 8920

NCC Education
The Towers
Towers Business Park
Wilmslow Road
Didsbury
Manchester
M20 2EZ
Tel: 0161 438 6200

The Institute of Data
Processing Management
(IDPM)
IDPM House
Edgington Way
Ruxley Corner
Sidcup
Kent
DA14 5HR
Tel: 0208 308 0747

The National Computing
Centre
Oxford House
Oxford Road
Manchester
M1 7ED
Tel: 0161 242 2499

Index